THE
8TH
HOUSE

also by Feng Sun Chen
Butcher's Tree (2012)

The 8th House

by Feng Sun Chen

Black Ocean
Boston · New York · Chicago

Black Ocean
P.O. Box 52030
Boston, MA 02205
blackocean.org

Cover Art and Illustrations by Josh Wallis | joshwallis.com
Book Design by Nikkita Cohoon | nikkita.co

ISBN 978-1-939568-08-3

Library of Congress Cataloging-in-Publication Data

Chen, Feng Sun, 1987-
  [Poems. Selections]
  The 8th house : poems / Feng Sun Chen.
     pages cm
  ISBN 978-1-939568-08-3 (alk. paper)
  I. Title.
  PS3603.H4475A6 2014
  811'.6-dc23

                              2014040168

FIRST EDITION

CONTENTS

I

[I AM THE MIDAS] 3

II

KINGDOM OF HEAVEN 65
ILLITERACY 68
DEAR READER, ... 69
STUPIDITY 70
ECSTASY 71
HOLY LAND 72
VISIONARY 73
PLAGUE OF IDIOTS 74
SIN EATER 75
SOUL 76
PRAYER 77
PRAYER 78
FAITH 79
HOW TO DIE 80
SENTENCES 81
LOVE IN THE VOID 82
WAR 83
SPIRIT 84
MADE IN CHINA 85
GRAMMAR OF TOUCH 90
TO LIVE 91

I AM THE MIDAS
OF SLOP
I AM THE MIDAS
OF BASILICA
I AM THE MIDAS
THAT TOUCHES EVERYTHING

THE ONLY ALL LOVING

THE ONLY ALL ENCOMPASSING

I AM THE MOTHER
THAT RUNS ON NOTHING
BUT THE POWER OF TRUE EQUALITY

THE FINE DUST

THE WORTH OF GOLD

IN ALL THAT I LOVE
IN ALL THAT I TOUCH

WITH MY HOARY FINGER

I CAN ENTER ANYTHING

A DAY IN THE LIFE OF A CONTEMPORARY PERSON

THE SWEETNESS OF EACH NOW DAY
STREAMING THROUGH THE SLANT

THE ORIENTAL CUNT
OF NORMAL TIME

THE MAGAZINE OF GOLDEN TEARS
AND ABRAHAM'S HEART
LEFT OUT IN THE MUD

I WAS THERE WHEN ABRAHAM STEPPED OUT OF THE
TRAIN
AND INTO THE MUD

I TOUCHED ABRAHAM WALLOWING
IN THE MOUND CYSTED MUD

WHEN THE DUST OF MARY
COATED YOUR FACE
I WAS THERE

AND I AM THE MIDAS
PUMPING THE TONGUE
MY HANDS ARE PRONGED WITH TONGUES

AND I LICK THE WORLD WE
I LICK THE HOUND WE

YOU ARE THE JUICE THAT DRAINS

I AM THE MIDAS
OF THE BRAIN

RICHNESS CULTURE OF ROT HOT WHAT I TOUCH
ROTS

MAKING IT FRESH
GETS ROTTEN

MAKING IT NEW
GETS OLD
MAKING IT IS OLD
GOLD
FRESH MEAT MESH

RECALL THESE STRANGE FRUITS

I PRECIPITATE TEXT
I WRITHE IN GOLDEN GEOLOGICAL SMEGMA

I TOUCH THE WATERS OF IN OUR BLADDER
I TOUCH THE WATERS OF IN OUR DUCT

THE SLEEP WAX IN OUR EYE
THICK WITH LIFE FILM

EVERYTHING TOUCH IS

IS IT

THE ELECTRIC SPIT
COURSES THROUGH ME
GIVES ME LIFE

I LIKE THE RUMPHOTMEAT

RATHER NOT SEE MY RACE
LOOKING BACK AT ME

I LIKE TO EAT OFF A MIRROR
AND PUT MY SNOUT TO IT

THE FINE DUST

THE TISSUE GALVANIZER

PEG THAT MEETS PEG LINKING

SNORT AND SLURP AND WRITHE DIGITALLY
DIGITS OF PITY

THE GOLD MEAT OF MY MURDERED DAUGHTER
WHOM I LOVE

AND WHO SHALL WITNESS MY LATERAL DESCENT
INTO REGURGITATED TEDIUM

AND WHO SHALL RIDDLE ME

INFECTIOUS RIDDLES
AND SOFT LIFE PUSTULATES

WHAT IS NOT UNCOMMON OF THE DOUBLE HEADED
AND THE DOUBLE MOUTHED

WHAT JOINS THE DAUGHTER AND THE FATHER THE
CAGE AND THE FIELD THE SLOTS AND THE STARHOLES
THE OLD LIGHT AND THE FRESH WOUND

CAUTION
CAUTION
DO NOT ENTER

LADIES GENTLEMEN HOUNDS

BABY PRODUCE UNISEX HANDICAPPED

GLISTENING BUTTERCUP OF CUT ARTERY JUST EMPTIED

WHITE GOLD OF THE ENMESHED TENDON JUNGLED
THROUGH A SLAT OF HOLY SAPIEN

ROSETTA OF RENDERED CITI
ZEN WRAPPED IN NEWSPRINT

LONGING TO TOUCH
THE THINGS IN THE MIRROR THE THINGS I LOVE THE
KILL I TENDERIZE I TRENCH I EAT

SO FRESH

SO RED

MARY

I REMEMBER WHEN WE SLAPPED EACH OTHER WITH
OUR RUMPS INSIDE THE MIRROR INSIDE THE BATH

THE ROOM WAS SO SQUARE

IT COULD NOT CONTAIN OUR MAGIC OUR MAGIC WAS
SO STRONG AND SO ELEMENTAL

I SUDDENLY THOUGHT I HAD GIVEN BIRTH

THERE WAS LOVE CASCADING THROUGH ME
FALLING FROM BONE
LOVE SO TENDER

AND WITH A PRICE

AND YOU RIP THE TAG FROM ME
LIKE FACE FROM FLESH

FACE HANGING FROM WINGS OF ADRENALINE

SHAME SHINY AND DISLOCATED AND GRATEFUL

BLOOMING BODY OR FLAYED FLOWER

The spirit does not survive

Now she is already dead

Born for the crate

Pure fat being with mammary and simultaneous craters

Hymn-shaped packed and honey infused pink in delicacy

It is a fine day when the soul wakes up and finds herself a Peg

I am happy about it

that my hymn tongue shall never touch the white or the pure

What she enters is already wounded

the terminology tube

She shall lay tiny eggs that shall not hatch but shall rot happily

Tiny revolts exit once a month from the poet

C.D. said Diego said that art is like ham

In the margins in the closet I said yes

I have noticed that ham cries juicy tears

The ham in the store, the ham in the crate, the ham before it was divided

Ham has a special wetness

The dead lover seeks wetness

She feels her aquatic genesis and the mixed wetness of things

that run through through

Through is the only direction to run

She loves all animals. She loves the wee openings of animals
and her wee friends who worry about the sincerity of their sloth.

She-ra said of the poet, it is a gay earth mother. The earth mother
also knows water, the monstergods that struggled out of the waterwomb.

He-man has a wetness of yearning. The water of his soul is a broth.
Inside him a brothel without customers.

Lately I have noticed the sound of groundwater.
It is a historical sound. Very moist and quiet and dripping.

The Peg can hear the dripping of the deep subterranean caves.

Zurita said of the Peg
offer up your body to be occupied by other bodies.

He carried the bodies of Chile like a rattle I could hear
the sands of bodies snaking through the head and out of the eyes.

This little Peggy went to the market.

Magma has a unique wetness.

It is a true wetness and it cries out like a farm animal.

Iris noted the slippery nature of evil. She said of the infertility of this country, it is an epidemic.

The earth is very pregnant and very pink. A crystal is pregnant for three months, three weeks, and three days.

Emptiness must die.

Don't open your body. It was already open.

But even if the tiny eggs are dead they must keep coming.

The magma of writing is slow as glass.

The fear of violence is a false fear
with its nature of singular drowned manatees
and it is mine and I am an elastic crystal filled
with manatee. I welcome you to us.

There is no violence unthinkable, no evil without ecology.
If only the manatees could heal together. The manatees swim
through the magma of the earth and are mistaken for mermaids.

This little Peggy stayed home.

Last night in a dream I sang a song of love to a brother
who must be mine. We were in camp and he wanted to die.

It is a basic life to crave so much the animated flesh of another.
If only I could sing the song continuously

throughout the whole nickel of the earth.
I have already forgotten the song. It was moving.

I am thankful for the Angel for he is not real
and has done what I cannot do.
The fish of his love swim through the bodies
of bodies and the bodies swim through the magma of him.

I am real and the reality of my reality
is as good as Spam.   .

And the wine of my water tastes like menstrual copper
and the bread of my life is refined.

I want to make you happy as a historical being but I have no power.
I am a poet and I do not survive. Let me be filled with your body.

Then I am filled like a curtain with not Mary but light.
The wetness of light is what I see drops from the mother.

Pegs are everywhere.

刀

When I see myself and feel shame it is a tiny part
of squatting before the endless eyeball of heaven

You push alligator clips inside me
The metal tips touch my immaculate conception

Nip nip
Buzz buzz

I remember the days of burning
Pleasurable peels white butter sheets

from my meek surface
I will die for my family

not because of shame
Only shame will propel me

to the depths of the ends of cavities
the ends of the deferens of dead teleology
over whom happily I will spread
my steaming shame

No designer shaped
the capacity of my dark sacs

I am being watched
even when the eyes
of the world have been burnt

in fact that is when I am most base

You agree with me, Angel
I expose by being exposed

Mother stews the blubber cubes for a long time in the ceramic pot. It is a pot that has been in the family for generations, and the pot is the color of human pig skin. Love and murder bubble androgynous thick tar mother stews the blub.

In the stew, cinnamon scrolls curl the anise stars haul the dark brown taste through the meat. The fatty cubes are soft and pink, and over time take on the color of dark anxiety inside the stew scroll. It is the flavor of years and time's passage and the sun's work on the black molecules hurling.

Disintegrating bits of lacy protein illustrate star-mom, a dimension measured by salt. The surprising mushroom of bone marrow at an opening of the skin after steaming, colony and cancer shaped, the stars of salt and motherfat stream down my chin and throat.

Life doesn't get away from ships and packing.
Who lies inside my whale belly?

Intestines of the real obscure
the gutless nothing of the holy.

The work of language for itself
dies inside.

Angels will tell you
that imagined things exist
but we do not imagine
what sits on the tongue.
Where does the creature exist
whom we have sacrificed?

The tolerant eye opens to a preserve of unlickable pink horror
so you are no longer used to making sense of forms.
The mud of the marrow is apparent in a pure instant.

The computer inside my whale meat wonders
how does post-orgasmic disgust?

Tiny spiders have laid eggs inside the mouthmatter door. They are not about to hatch. They may never hatch. They brood and grow. I don't miss my friend, but I almost miss being a sentient ham.

Danger lies in the solidity of lymph, of potential,
of dreams amassed not under the sun but in its obstruction.

Rather than the outflux of thousands of pale spiders, swaddling them inside a shell of maryskin, fear the bonding agent.

I hold a thousand thresholds at my threshold.

Mother looks like thousands of other mothers, my father in black and white, all his features gray, I cannot see him, may never hatch.

At the museum of purity, the groomed watch six hours of Empire, slicing up chunks of time.

Pegs cling to the shuttle. There is no machine perfect enough to hold soft bodies.

Soft bodies wield knives.

No organism is ashamed under the knife.

An expression of something I pin
on your cheekbone sprouts cystic.

A pidgin bleeds with reflected sunlight.
The pure bottom of light revives.

Reduction makes better transformation.

All this mary could boil
down to a pity of one nation.

The star bends into its yellow nothingness
clad on all sides by ink black fat.

There is only one mind of pain.

You can feel it when you walk though it, mary said, like
walking through a cloud.

Sometimes the forms bite each other.

I am a Peggy and I need you. Ingots will hatch and cocoon you in the silk
of my appreciation. The truffle struggles to be set free. Someday the end
will have come.

Animals are the common ground.
Why are we walking through this grid?
"Everything is personal."

It will not be one hero that saves us, it was never.

The pink brown wilderness in the farrowing
cannot turn around or move.
They shudder like jelly in jelly molds,
translucent comets coagulating inside
among the flower noises.
They know they are meant to be jade.

Mother is filling up
dumplings with curds
of pork and cabbage.

Grandmother makes
the most transcendent
pork stew. She says

it is the secret
to longevity. The texture
of browned skin
and its rendering.

刀

Before life became a gyro under a grater
snowing a salty brown snow,

"Time is not a straight line,
but just a flat hell, like a desert. I am a tomb
robber who is robbing my own tomb.
Things from my tomb are exhibited under the radiant sun.
Every time it happens I feel crude."

At the bottom of the ocean inside a metallic shell.

At the top of a mountain which whispers inside-out.

In the belly of a natural event that does not want to take you higher.

In the eye of a gravity I break with you out of earth.

Suffering unimaginable,

love eternal,

the double helix of attention.

To see, then the radiant dead

nourished to us.

I became an American in high school.
Through the seven subjections and homerooms
I felt the glory of the Lord.

We called animal control over a rabbit with a broken leg.
He said that squirrels made him angry because they skittered.

We drove past Target and the abandoned factory and the ice rink.
We drove past the cemetery past Paradise High.

I thought about the hairs on my chinny chin chin.

When Jasmine got her Brazilian,
she looked like a plucked chicken.

He liked hair and he had body odor like Mexican fast food
and we fatted each other in the father's minivan and the music room
and the bathroom and any room without a bed.

We drove past the nature preserve and past the new mall and
went to the zoo. I didn't care that I cared about the way he treated me.
We fatted on the rail and looked at the potbellied Pegs and the penguins.

He wanted constant praise and I was happy to fat him.
Good listening brightens the eyes.
To sing of love, sugar, and homeland
is to come into allegiance.

He made a lot of noise and had big lungs and this created the illusion
of something, and I believed in his white liberalism.
My purity was insecurity.

We rode the rail all over the zoo.

"I put the disease of this world and my sick body together."

I put the disease of the world and my sick body together.

It wasn't his fault when he shot himself. There was mary all over the
     floor and linen.

He could hear the collective subfrequencies of crying animals.

The mind of god was mary and gurgling fat.

When he called me to tell me he was addicted to Japanese porn
I was driving past Cub Foods on my way to Ikea to get lamps
that looked like amniotic lanterns. Help me, the rapist said,
I'm being hoisted up.

They came with knives and mirrors.

You can render pork, have pork, have a pork, pork a pork, pork a man
or a pork, both having porks, observe porks, cook pork, sear pork,
eat pork, cut pork, analyze pork.

Fat is malleable and a potent source of energy.

mary was organic and pure. She wore jeans in the summer. She believed
in love and gave birth to a void.
She is why we believe in love among creation.
Pegs have very similar organs to human beings, she said, having never
    tasted a Peg or a pork.

There was fire in my loins and all the world
was wrapped in glistening fat.
All I wanted, I still want.

I still want to be filled with the richest light.

I am not a vegetarian but I have a sympathy with meat.

I sit in my room alone and they hang about me like friends.

They are my true friends.

I have true friends the way a body has a soul.

I have meat the way a body has network.

The way a network has psychosis.

The way corpses have no body. The way souls have mechanism.

I love them openly and we hold nothing back and the weight of our
    agreement breaks my back.

I lie here cut in half as the spinal lubricant shines
out of me out of my nose and soul.

We are the flowering mass, thousands of us. Machines
make music, but the soft monster does not fit.

I am the folds of a curdling rose whose factory smashes the glass.
Soft meadows absorb the snap of bulky souls.

The foam on the sea made of dead
mermaids still smoking like fish
black jelly of dreams
joins sky and sea
and the birds blacken and lay with the fish
and the beans are filled with sea
pink oceans full of nude mollusks.
They are making the great journey
back to the dark soup.
We sputter like metal lobsters to the beach
gigantic and impotent
blissed on deformed sperm
pained eggs and homunculus love.
I am desperate for a fetus.
To be a soft stomach bloated with sea life
cannibalistic like a virgin.
I will walk on the black shore with my child
still shiny with mucus and blind
a plant made of flesh
and the foam of the dead
jelly of a double hell which holds
and makes us possible.

Through the snail gait of mary tinged lymph,
the hairs of sentimentality spread apart.

One eyed needle pumped its art
into cauliflower nerves
waving signs protesting nothing.

Nothing is stronger than a pain-net,
the green grapes shining
high over the rubber fox

All in the business of amnesia,
when I could call myself an element
crushing mary's hand.

Gazing up at laminated paradise,
white beach palm tree destiny lines
see the gaping red porn of my contact.

See panic flatten out.
See mary run.
See dark lymph flood from purity into purity.

I held mary in my arms and her eyes were shutting
her eyelids dew without the grass
mary slipped through my fingers
dried into gray crust.

I slowly remembered the brown ring around your moon
black moon
orificial star.

mary flows through the black moon.

mary is condemned to live
in the rabbit milk globe of the moon
to make medicine.

I held mary in my arms
it was hard to walk.

I watch mother again walk through
the thick viscosity of wood
one leg jutted.

The woods reduce her she drips through
pages, water astonishing and difficult.

This kind of slow
make by squeezing
within the cut
and slender joint alone.

One sign of possession is not to recognize
yourself in the mirror.
Another to look out the window
see the island of your personal exile on fire.

Everyone a meditation
with no clothes rising from ashes.

Where I come from, even my nipples
loved to speak English.

Is that why
since moving here
I have become unrecognizable
and mother mary has stopped loving me?

Now let little Peggy discern these islands of time.
Is it manageable?
In times of richness and spectacular water of strawberry eyes
meat is preserved is perforated not performed.

Heat can have color. Nebula can have color. No color exists
before the color. No pain before the pain.

There is asking, a masking between voices or voids,
how can a stone be a void? In the way I am stone and void.

I am not a witness. The bug has eyes is filled
with eyes it is a blurry world that licks these eyes.
Gathers salt on these eyes.

I fetishize eyes. Lidded holes in the face little souls
in the mace. I identify through these blue blue globes.

I am not a witness but a wet mess.

Mom, isn't the wetness of cruelty a witness?
When I excrete transparent tears of joy, when I weep
gunk water by the fire of my chinny chin chin I weep
from a place of darkness dressed as houses.

If I could feel this light for you if I could be good if I could.

I put a tissue on the face of mary.

刀

Is it because we have two eyes that we can only see two things?
Because I am alive that I am the measure of all things?
Then it is time to die.

I must think too much. Silence worth more than a pretty
tinkling yellow charm petroleum
and more than what I can say about any one of my brilliant mothers
under whom I writhe and cry out my written memories
given to me by Abraham.

Almost done, I make this line reach the edge
of the page to manifest destiny
where shores of no page will lap at edge of Peg feet
scaly feet with pores underneath each scale
hold up giant exposed spinal cords of gigantic nerve rings.
I beckon for you to jump through the nerve ring.
You are tiger with a mane and face of a monkey.

Purely rational beings are close in size to potatoes
replete with microbes and worm ring.

In the night I curl up in your tasty charity.

A woman body is an angel factory.
In afternoon I come home, turn on the tube,
and relax into shiny squares of children singing.
I cry into mouths of exploited angels.

Each pore of my body blubbers open and tries to grow teeth.
All the boys in my choir have your nerveface.
Boys within my boy all the Pegs in my body like white snowflakes.

In the night I am a sprawling sea coral
inch long cherubs unravel from my sponge nerves.
Somehow I, a burned mummy, am responsible for war.

Into the toiletplant I water.

Hair water flutters in the mary.

I water my mouthplant.

Mouthplant water the meatplant.

Nourishment from mouth water
swum up the stalk to cavity plant.

Plant speak is not like the color virgin or smoothness of budding stalk.
Plant speak is startled nerve ending in halved molar.

Illegitimate ghost genitalia fall gently from plant lips.
The ghost buds whisper and scream like the cutest gout.

How can I disappear and love you all at once?

I tuck objects in my fatty cracks underbelly cranberries
my honey baked mum an accidental planetarium

displaced springtime have rotted and hung themselves
in the vast vastness her starholes sprout strange dry stalks

that wintering that shrivel lip peal under salt
battleship planetary balconies of salt

when I touch her with my inside-out ear I hear
platters of unidentified flying objects,
the type of love that is packed

that is void and miniscule that wants
to be smashed between mattresses

I know I will fail as I do
in all that I do.

Communication is an ugly word.
It is not pretty like Peggy.

A Peg is more sincere than I could ever be.
A Peg squeals without self-consciousness or self esteem.
When teeth sink into the Peg the Peg accepts it and the Peg body performs
the dark meat ripple as a whole like a pink pond.

Why do I have future cancer and now ache and when I am in love.

Shame is body grazing death. The Peg wakes up in the morning and dies
throughout the working day. I am putting a star inside her, a star that
hurts from the future, a future that hurts from the present stippled by
antebellum legacies.

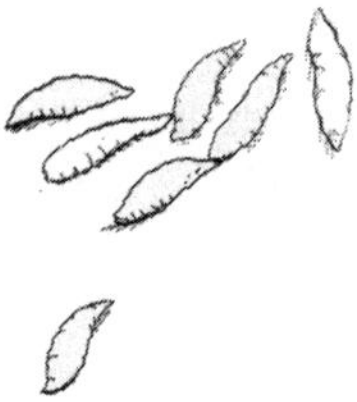

刀

I am a Peg when I copulate.
It is difficult to be sincere while Pegulating.
The ghost of my humanity polices my milky
being like sties in the edges of the eye. I am
in love and it feels like flesh in flight.
When I am in the stinking spasm of love
swimming in a white mud pool of cupids
filling the creases in bodies
why is it that when I am in love
I feel as if I am visiting a memorial
and the tiny deformed frogs of war atrocities
as if they were a special kind of atrocity
leap and swarm over deformed frogs
at the bottom of the pool
loss becomes mythical in scope like god
I need you to close your camel human eyes
while we tread thick water over the sea of radical frogs.
It is too late and I have heard things
there is salt in the heart that rots.
Already the rot has taken hold
the hungry rot eaters are stirring in their cell membranes
desire redgorged like an eye between
the sea confused with heat
the sea without integrity.

The ghost of my humanity polices my milky being
like sties in the edges of the eye.
I am in love and it feels like flesh
in flight. When I am in the stinking spasm
of love swimming in a white mud pool of cupids
that fill the creases of bodies why
is it that when I am in love I feel as if
I am visiting a memorial
and the tiny deformed frogs of war atrocities
as if they were a special kind of atrocity
leap and swarm over the deformed frogs
at the bottom of the pool
and loss becomes mythical in scope like god.
You are such a good person good for nothing
in a swine world where persons are precarious
where the dead are looking.
I want to protect our humility from every thing.
I need you to close your camel human eyes
in the darkness it opens to infinite centers.

I fold my brothers into my decay.

I have hated my Chinese mother because I hated myself
and hate is the kind of love that speaks about itself.

My love, I tumbled in the magma of filth to rid.

It is customary for the star to be sliced such that
its shit re-enters the star we make into our meal

and it is the place of love to clean
to bleed and clean and receive the dead.

I don't want to be loved because I want to be loved
still among the still.

Tongues have language before language
the sow's writhing is clear and clearer than language

like I grip my own Peg and rub it and cum clear bile

The pork tries
it tries very hard.

Now she is already dead.

This little Peggy had fun.

This little Peggy had none.

What does a Peggy Do
A Peggy does not interpret
A Peggy is of the trufflepimpled
earth and marbled river
A Peggy translates even upon its own emesis
inside the gestation barrels wheelbarrow fate
Even upon the homesick rabbitrumpled moon the Peg translates
The Lifesac begins its dreamy strawberry lozenge production
Fellow Trinkets!
We may simmer each other in Asian sauces and A1 sauces
and receive each other on the tongue with the wine
our industry of slaughter is fecund
and the Peggy winks through the contraption
A Peggy is affectionate
Jelly & Veal
Peggy can be tree
Peggy can be rat
Peggy can be earth
Peggy can be succulent
And I continue to learn as the world falls through me
Ham can be sweet like jam
Ham can be honeyed
Ham loves the light of darkness
And Ham said unto the disgraced sailors
you will eat of yourselves and never leave this island
The justice of the ham is a ham
You can be a piece of Ham and the whole world laughs with you
Nobody really eats ham
When you truly eat of ham
You will not survive the feast
The Three Little Pegs is a love story

What story isn't about longing
Even a story with no plot is about longing
Perhaps it has forgotten what it longs for
long before what we have forgotten is forgot
That is what I learned from my adventures with various types of ham
And I continue to learn as this world falls through me
I mince the ham of holy light
and the grease of Abraham
as I bite the vulva of the star in the next stall
this world falls

II

KINGDOM OF HEAVEN

Now that my love has turned around and I can see his evil face
I have thrown up dogs and cats representing sorrow.
When I pick up a book and open it, it is dead.
I cannot feel when I read the interior design
of the refined soul
and even the ugly poem is refined.
Oliver, what can you do for me as a gingery dream,
the sweetest of white boys
can conspire with me and my triangulated support
of their violent home improvement.
There is nothing you can do for me.
I can no longer write from the soul
because this is my soul now,
the landscape is fertile and I am in exile.
United garbage of the world,
what can I do for me and what can I do for you,
how do I know the beauty of the world,
how can I show yourselves
when you are trapped inside a grand maison?
What can I stand?
I stand for the ones who are lying down I stand
for my asexual thunder
the instant stream
stops time and halts the black gauze carriage.
Is it different when you step in?
The instant cannot flow
The center cannot hold
Soft butcher soft femme soft devotional butcher
soft pain soft radish soft radical sex water

When I take you in the water is frozen but we fall throughout.
You are a downtrodden rainbow of abuses and mistakes
and the most gorgeous of reflectors.
Baby toaster, sparks flying, your body sputters
set fire to my hair and clothes
slowly the mechanics break.
Everybody has a heart but I do not
I have an academic wound and a hungry soul
I have a stomach that touches
envelops your rusty pink box
you are a coughing divinity wrapped in hydrochloric acid
my coughing heart
I fill in the cracks.
Power surges.

I came into this world to love you but I was born
without the organ of love.

During lovemaking there is a funny stuttering noise in the hole
and you realize that holography is the absent response
and every hyperglorified technological advance is a congenital failure.

ILLITERACY

mary will accept the obliterative.
mary will accept the sweet cold nodes of the cables.
Operator operator
The holes in your text seem to signify some kind of terror
which I see as the backside of erasure, if you should ask what the other
side of an eraser is.
When I am a pale man I drag my luggage in a suit
and its coarse hairs fluctuate
in the air conditioned wasteland of future ruin.

DEAR READER,

Ghosts are more powerful than fathers because they are pure surface,
layers upon hysteric layers of surface.
The ambiance of your dying skin besieges me. With such illiteracy
I hope to reach the dead within you.

STUPIDITY

the screen is more skin where skin folds
if gravity inside has pulled / puckered growth
Isabella showed me how primates sex it without thumbs
you put your superglow in me
the virus breaks in kubla khan
a stately pleasure doesn't slit the slit
inside you are planets like panic on epic time
and I am the hexagonal earthsuckling ring

ECSTASY

I see now Isabella, firearms whirling like Christian flesh
I am the earth that meshed
know the plague is real, this small part
will grow upthreaded static shoot in javelins of light
I no longer speak as cervix opens its humic mouth
I yearn towards the tipping sun
one gigantic flaming thumb
before which I am stupid and before which you stumble
naked through the bush like
is our soul disfigured?
is my soul disfigured?
What is the figure of a soul inside everything
that is my body shitting discreet into the porcelain structure?
I am ungracefully grateful for the genteel friendships in my life
in spite of my fear of shallow waters.

HOLY LAND

I trust that your faith in me is deep, sister.
I trust that my faith in you is deep as well.

The animal scratches the surface of the earth.

Flat as earth is real,
it is the smooth, godly surface I touch gingerly as an organ's tip.
Felled by electric divinity

We are cast away from a world of dying spirits into a new one.
Your spirit dies gracefully
down in the clay where spirits collide greasily
traveling on crude geology.

My love must be smaller than the smallest amino acid.
Is there room on earth for us?

The tiniest love must hold massive pillars of destruction.
The tiniest muscle of it tweaks a neuron in the brain.
My father opens the door,
mistakes the sound of leaves for rain
and carries my groceries to the car.

VISIONARY

Fee demands a reading
the fluid cannot go above the line that means you are a beast.
Jesus came back a soft monkey,
Did u have sex with him mary? Did mary come out of your hole?
Did mary dry up with the cotton to make the shape of sanity?
Test my entity, my hand is clammy with old butter
that is spread across the weak. I see mary high up.
She is glowing with many linen lips. She falls down to us.
Large appendages touch her, mary
wanting to swallow the beaten figures within us.

PLAGUE OF IDIOTS

I like it when you look at me with disdain.
I say things that make you want to hurt me.
This is the real thing, severe as winter
part icicle that cannot be smashed another
part that parts leaves nothing to fill, only futility fills.

I don't believe in emptiness, but when you look in my eyes
what do you see?
To want filth to want decay is the longest tradition.
I rule the belt, unfurl the belt.
It puts all my earnings to the test.

SIN EATER

Sunflower looks up
The crane lifts
I take
Whatever you give
You place
The machine in me

SOUL

You put your machine in me.
I want it to run and cheat.
My hare bunny squeals.
The house I live in is a house of truth and punishment.
I killed discipline. I killed distance. Now it opens
the wet brook of my face.
Now we grow from its tears.
When I stab it, it stabs me.

PRAYER

I want someone to watch me
pick the dirt under my fingernails
to watch as I smell it
to watch as I look hideous in the morning sun
the pores in my face crying out
prematurely for maggot seeds
to see the grotesque meaning of my body
to look into my blind eyes and show me
how I am no more

PRAYER

When I look at you I wonder if my eye slits look retarded
if I taste like the pig anuses ground into my sweet sausage at dinner
only when I look at you do I become a written person
I would rather die
but I want to have a life so I look and become
a betrayer of the animal in us
swimming like souls in purgatory muck

FAITH

The doctor swabbed the face of an angel and it hurt.

Bloodwork done, vials of plasma
will tell me about history and the universe.

Viruses have something to tell you.
Something dark and secret.
The way our bodies were never ours.

Our bodies belong to evil, cruelty, the Sun.
Only the ways our bodies are broken belong to us.

In this way my diseases make me real.

A river of pus is my love of the world,
shifting plates and inarticulate conversations,
vulnerability in the twelfth house.

I am my father
inside my mother.

I have to go away now.
I have to go away as I retreat into angelic flesh.

I don't eat grapefruit.
I don't eat milk.

Children don't ask where these things come from.
It's a lot worse than where babies come from.
I don't ask either
where souls are made.

After so long, I believe in demons because I saw one.
It was weak from pain, a universe of pain
lying next to me.

I felt for it
and stroked its face.

HOW TO DIE

I am a nation in its feminine form, prostrate
desperately seeking the love of its citizens.
Impossible to give love to a nation that does not love
how would you accept it?
Only in the vertical wall of its dead
who also sought the end of times.
In my excessive romance novel of unrequited love I enact
the tragedy of man's pursuit of nationhood.
I slice the pussy back into history.
I am the nothingness that reeks of man's origin in the fishy
Light-absorbing bed of the sea and its watery earth
even my vulnerability and passivity barely receive
the footsteps of ghosts that have no weight.
Why worry about the dead when the living are dead?
I want to reach
the dead within you
the place among the animals
the bones made of the bones of endless beginning.
I never want to write again.
I want to touch your cunt in the long night that will also never end.

SENTENCES

Broken sentimentality reads like a bar of chocolate
pocky sticks deliciously fitting into the smallest mouth

I come upfront to no one
to the death in all of you

with the secret that I am a body of Chinese hamsters
with tiny holes for chocolate snax

if I am not fed I die, so I do
hundreds of times a minute a hundred hamsters die

the real hamsters in me surround me at all times
and they surround you

when you perceive the hairs around my dark asterix each one standing
for an eternity of shame

inscribed by invisible carriers
I know you but I hope you are surprised at how the hole does not

belong to you
because it does

syntax should die

I see your lies, your beauty, the misogyny that makes me cum
over smashed rodents the dried crust that is the commonplace

in the hair of all our feeling

LOVE IN THE VOID

Hollow is the ponderous wake

Suddenly I have insides that have contacted me, they say mary

I am their birth mother and they have been looking for me a long time

The baby in me expects u to feed me like a chinese mother

I am lying on the ground becoming more and more flat

I carry a wake from all corners mary hits me

I am not every woman but I am every hurtle from a high place

merrily merrily merrily merrily merrily merrily

WAR

Precarity is the center of density
it is the center of the stupid within
the opacity of sense

Stupid is precarious
the stutter verges on the 8th house
when I become unrecognizable as a person

The machine inside me
precipitates stupidly
stupid is the face of Orpheus as he turns around
stupid is the face of Eurydice as she lifts her face like an object
the instance of loss is lost to us

Stupid is my regard of the desirable body
I want to die into the crushing precarity of its mass
my precarious ethnicity does not vibrate
as much as the fraying chords inside me

Computers are the stupidest
I grab its stupid cock
I smash it
inside the stuff blooms out like a dimension of gauze
woven through it is the invitation
I accept it
every capillary of my unformed organism unfurls to collect on it

Outside of this attention is disappointment
the darkness inside me turns and turns

SPIRIT

the slice that comes an angel remembers me

slice that come like acid

now that I can make phrasing

I kill the layer that touches what is without me

my touch of the air is now pure

my tongue of maim

aims no awl

you touch my kant

touch it with my hand

I am killing the wholesome to know without knowing so that

my dumbabyness can grow

huge grow wings arms pieces

so it can hold your hauntedness

so that I may survive hauntedness

MADE IN CHINA

no ledge without power

no I won't go to your exhibition

no I will not forget

no I cannot remember

no I will never learn

but I know things

I don't know any thing

I am learning

the force of my stupidity

guides me

interstitial forces

the force of a hand

a damaged eye

the wax in the ear

ecstatic skin

the skin that belongs to the green, red

when the skin is broken

the body knows

the body's deep stupidity

my soul's humility

knows but I don't know

I am never outside

but I am near

open to you

close to you

always inside

my face carries

my head is the carrier

to be close like a naked skin

the metaphor of history

that I misremember

being dumb

I cut

like the fissure

in the rectum

of my lover

I am the thing

you are always about

to see

even I don't know

the extent of my mother's

amnesia

the baldness of my grandmother

the failure

of my thesis

how does anything actually

reconfigure kinship

is kin the skin without plurality

is blood the commons

am I a pig

for my vague trauma

my fear

my alien antennae

your fear of contamination

the truth of

my android lover

her plastic cunt

her dark skin

the receipts in my bag

what I have stolen

the intense light

of dying stars

the soul

in my computer

the assembly

of slave bodies

living in space

the blank that does not translate

between mediums

between lines

what's love

can I know

you beyond

my wrong my stupid

language?

GRAMMAR OF TOUCH

when the swallow constricts
I swallow my mother
acid pink film moves fields
brick of your supreme kin
flat organ
remember pilgrims
palm sounds
blush fronds
you commit
beside horror
compression is
oriental
muscle licks
brain stems
dream breaks
rock dams
the roaring roar
stops never
what it is to live
crashes in me
endurance fattens
enzyme
the pull
I take

TO LIVE

The swarm of the crowd is not a question of its intelligence

Dead crowds go to the arboretum and the stadium
plastered with the faces of dead soldiers

My bladder is bursting and when I pee into the lonely toilet
that works to sustain a broken crowd thru phobia and magic pollution

I come into nonexistence

Then I lie down and imagine the same feeling of disappearance into
commonality

This impossible baby dream with tiny fingers and toes

I try to remember being born

To remember being connected by flesh to another flesh

How interesting the difficulty is in taking back the commons

In taking back acts of touch

How interesting my desire to be destroyed

Materialism hates materialism

My privilege to be fucked

And sucked into a blizzard of consumption to sustain this fucking

It is stupid to escape the self

The real self wants to be ruptured

Sex never happens between the lines

Where can a heart go? Can a target spiky and throbbing with weaponry
turn its arrows into a technology for walking? So pierced

So heavy

I want blood to splatter from my mouth when I speak

Because sharing is caring

And shame is a mechanism for individuation

So is self-esteem

The lyric will come back a zombie

When will the crowd wake up?

So many ambassadors of the other world scream for you

You are covered in our blood

So many ambassadors of another world scream for us

We are covered in its blood

ACKNOWLEDGEMENTS

Thanks to Kim Hyesoon for some quoted lyric matter, thanks to my sisters of the 12th House, and thanks to the gods, spirits and creatures who have taken care of me.